Three
from Scotland

Contents

Retold by Tony Mitton
Illustrated by Joe Rice

Collins Educational
An Imprint of HarperCollins*Publishers*

Greyfriars' Bobby

A true story

Jock, the old shepherd, walked
sadly away from the hill-farm.
He was in no hurry. He was
too old now to be a useful
shepherd, so the farmer had paid
him his last wages and told him
to go.

Now he was on his way to the city
of Edinburgh, to struggle along as
best he could during the last years
of his life. He'd only gone a short
way when he heard barking behind
him, and turned to see an eager ball
of fur leap up at him.

It was Bobby, the little terrier that belonged to Elsie, the farmer's daughter. Bobby had never liked being Elsie's dog. He didn't like being cuddled, and he didn't like being kept indoors.

As far as Bobby was concerned, Old Jock was his master. His place was out in the open at his master's heels.

Now that Old Jock was leaving,
Bobby wanted to go with him.

"Be off with you Bobby. Go back.
Go back home."

But, try as he might, the old
shepherd could not get Bobby to
go back. So he just trudged on, glad
of Bobby's company, while the dog
followed him all the way to the old
city of Edinburgh.

When Old Jock got to the city, he found cheap lodgings. He spent his days sitting around in the market place, and his evenings by the fire in his favourite inn.

But winter was on its way and, before long, the cold, wet weather had begun to make him ill. Old Jock took to his bed and faithful Bobby stood guard over his master.

Old Jock grew weaker. His life was coming to an end. At last, he died, and his landlady arranged a funeral.

Bobby stayed close to his master's side. Even when the coffin was carried to Greyfriars' Churchyard he would not be parted from it.

As the gravediggers walked away, the small dog moved even closer, to watch over his master's grave.

Dogs were not allowed in the cemetery, but Mr Brown, the caretaker, could not keep him out.

From that day, Bobby was a familiar sight in Greyfriars' Churchyard.

Whatever happened, Bobby would always come back to his master's grave at night-time and, in the end, Mr Brown grew very fond of him.

When the city council started to round up the stray dogs, it looked as if Bobby might be taken away. But the poor children from round about loved Bobby, and managed to scrape together enough money to buy him a licence.

Even the Lord Provost was so moved by Bobby's story that he granted him the "Freedom of the City" which meant that Bobby was an honoured guest in the city and could go wherever he pleased.

Soon Bobby was famous all over
Edinburgh, and people in other
parts of the country heard the
story of how the faithful little dog
guarded his master's grave.
Eventually, when Bobby died, a
monument was raised to him.

The monument is a drinking fountain with an upper and a lower basin where both people and animals can stop to take a drink of water.

At the top is a statue of the little terrier, sitting up as keenly as ever. The statue is still there today, not far from the grave of Old Jock.

The Seal Hunter
A folk tale

There was once
a fisherman
who lived near
John O'Groats.
At first he
made his living
by catching salmon and cod, but he
soon found that he could make
a lot of money hunting seals for
their skins.

In those days people used sealskins
to make warm clothing, and they
came from far and wide to buy
them from him.

The fisherman grew so rich he was
able to give up fishing altogether.

He had become a very skilful hunter, but one day he tried to kill a very large old seal that lay on a ledge of rock. As he stuck his knife into the seal, it let out a great cry and leaped into the water. The seal disappeared below the waves.

That evening a tall, dark stranger knocked at the hunter's door. The stranger asked the hunter to go with him to his master's house. He said that his master wanted to buy many skins and would pay him well.

The two men bundled up the skins on the stranger's great black horse and then galloped through the dusk at amazing speed. The hunter felt as though he was flying through the air.

Before long they came to a cliff
edge. The stranger said, "We're
nearly there." This puzzled the
hunter, as there was no sign of a
house nearby. The stranger got off
the horse and walked towards the
cliff edge, beckoning the hunter
to follow.

The hunter found himself looking
down at the grey sea far below.

"Where is your master's house?"
he asked, bewildered.
"Here, my friend, here!" said the
stranger suddenly.

And he grasped the hunter firmly
round the waist and leaped off the
cliff. The two men fell, until they
splashed into the cold, grey sea.
Down and further down they went,
into the blackness.

As the hunter turned to grasp the stranger's hand, he saw that his guide had become a beautiful, graceful seal. Together they floated through greeny light towards a white underwater palace at the edge of a huge, undersea forest.

As they swam into the palace the
hunter heard a terrible wailing.
The cavern was filled with seals.
And they were weeping, filling the
palace with their terrible sadness.

And there, lying on a rock, was a
large, old seal. Sticking out of the
old seal's side, was the handle
of the hunter's knife.

When he saw it the hunter was filled with fear and shame. He knew that this was the seal he had killed. He fell to his knees and begged for mercy and forgiveness.

"Do not be afraid," said his seal guide quietly. "We will not harm you. This is my father, our leader, and only you can save him."

"How?" asked the hunter. "What must I do?"

"Pull the knife from his side and smooth the wound with your hand," explained the seal. "Then he will live again."

The hunter did as he was asked and the old seal rose slowly from the rock. The company of seals fell silent.

"I am the King of the Seal People and you have given me back my life," said the seal. "In return I will allow you to keep yours. But you must never hunt a seal again. If you do, it will bring death to you.

"You must become a fisherman once more. Then the seal folk will always be your friends and your nets will never be empty. Will you make this promise?"

"I promise," said the hunter, putting his knife away in its sheath. He felt his seal-guide pulling him back toward the door. They floated upwards through the blackness, rising until they broke above the surface of the grey sea.

As they bobbed up into the air, the hunter saw that his guide was once again the dark stranger. The stranger stretched out an arm and swept at a passing wave. Instantly, the great black horse sprang up out of it and they mounted, as before.

The black horse galloped away, flying up over the cliff-top and towards the hunter's cottage. The horse stopped by the gate to let the hunter down. As his feet touched the ground, the great horse wheeled round and galloped towards the sea with the dark seal-man on its back.

The hunter went slowly into his
cottage. He unbuckled his knife belt
and hung it up on the wall as a
reminder never to hunt seals again.
From that day on his nets were
always full of fish so, although
he was no longer rich, he never
went hungry.

Jack and the Thorn Bush
A fable

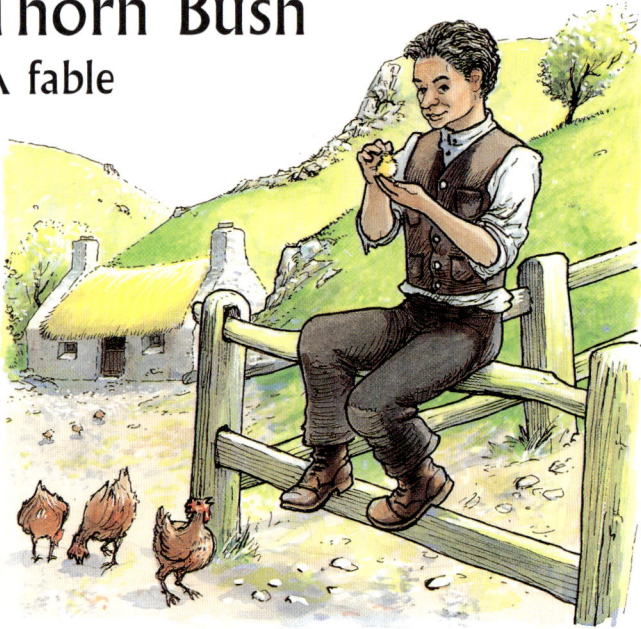

This is the story of young Jack who lived with his old mother in a croft in the Highlands.

Things weren't going well for them as their crops weren't growing, the hens weren't laying, and now the cow's milk had dried up.

Jack was a kind lad. But he wasn't very bright and he was a bit lazy.

One day his mother turned to him and said, "Jack, I'm not as young as I used to be, but you're a young, strong lad and you should be working hard. You can start tomorrow by taking the cow to market to sell her. Buy me a roll of cloth, too. I'm all in rags and it's time I made myself a dress to wear."

So the next day Jack took the cow to market. He sold her for a few pounds, did some shopping with the money and bought a roll of cloth for his mother.

Then he decided to call at the inn to have a chat with some of the other crofters. He stayed rather a long time, and when he set out for home it was late at night and very dark.

It was a cold night, for the wind was blowing strong and chill. The moon was hidden behind the clouds and it was raining, so it was hard to see the road ahead.

About half way up the hill that led to his croft he passed a thorn bush that creaked in the wind. He walked up to it and, well, it was dark, he was tired, and what with the size and shape of it and its funny little creaking noise, he mistook the bush for a poor old woman with nowhere to go.

"This is no night for a poor old woman like yourself to be out in the cold," said Jack kindly. "Come back with me to our croft and warm yourself by the fire."

But the old woman (being a thorn bush) just would not be moved.

Jack tried to persuade her, but when he put his arm around her to lift her he got pricked by the thorns. He thought it was the old woman scratching him out of anger.

"That's it," thought Jack. "If she won't come, she won't come."

He took the roll of cloth and gently wrapped it around the thorn bush. "That should keep her warm," he thought. "I'll come back for my mother's cloth in the morning."

The next morning his mother woke
him up. "You've got the shopping
I see," she said, "but did you
remember the cloth?" So Jack told
her about the creaky old woman
and the cloth.
"I'll go down after breakfast to fetch
it," he promised.

When Jack got down to the hill to
the thorn bush he realised his
mistake. The thorns on the bush had
ripped the cloth to tatters.

He was so angry with the bush that he decided to dig it up. As he pulled up the bush, he noticed an old wooden box, down in the hole. He opened it up to find that it was crammed with gold and silver coins.

He ran to show the box to his mother. "Our troubles are over, Jack," she cried. "With this money we can live well for the rest of our days." But as she spoke Jack was off and out the door with the spade in his hand. "Where are you off to now?" she called after him.

"It's the thorn bush, mother," he said. "I can't just leave it to die there on the hillside after the good it's brought us." And Jack went out and replanted the creaky thorn bush.

It soon took root again and was in blossom before long. The bush flourished and so did Jack and his mother in their croft on the Scottish Highlands.